VENUS

The Hot and Toxic Planet

by Ellen Lawrence

Consultants:

Suzy Gazlay, MA
Recipient, Presidential Award for Excellence in Science Teaching

Kevin Yates
Fellow of the Royal Astronomical Society

Published in 2014 by Ruby Tuesday Books Ltd.

Editor: Mark J. Sachner
Designer: Emma Randall

Photo Credits:
NASA: Cover, 6, 8, 9 (top left), 10, 11 (bottom), 14–15,
16–17, 18–19, 20–21; NASA and Ruby Tuesday Books:
12–13; Ruby Tuesday Books: 7, 22; Shutterstock: 9
(bottom), 11 (top); Superstock: 4–5, 9 (top right).

Library of Congress Control Number: 2013939981

ISBN 978-1-909673-04-5

Printed and published in the United States of America

For further information including rights and
permissions requests, please contact our Customer
Service Department at 877-337-8577.

Contents

Words shown in **bold** in the text are
explained in the glossary.

Welcome to Venus

Imagine a scorching hot world that is millions of miles from Earth.

The land is rocky, and there are more than 1,000 **volcanoes**.

It is daytime, but it looks like night.

That's because a thick layer of clouds and poisonous **gases** blocks out the Sun's light.

Welcome to the **planet** Venus!

Spacecraft have visited Venus. They sent information about the planet back to scientists on Earth. This picture was created on a computer using that information. It shows how the surface of Venus might look.

A human could not survive on Venus. It is too hot, and the **toxic**, or poisonous, gases would be deadly to any living thing.

Toxic clouds and gases

The Solar System

Venus is moving through space at about 78,000 miles per hour (126,000 km/h).

It is moving in a big circle around the Sun.

Venus is one of eight planets circling the Sun.

The planets are called Mercury, Venus, our home planet Earth, Mars, Jupiter, Saturn, Uranus, and Neptune.

Icy **comets** and large rocks, called **asteroids**, are also moving around the Sun.

Together, the Sun, the planets, and other space objects are called the **solar system**.

Most of the asteroids in the solar system are in a ring called the asteroid belt.

An asteroid

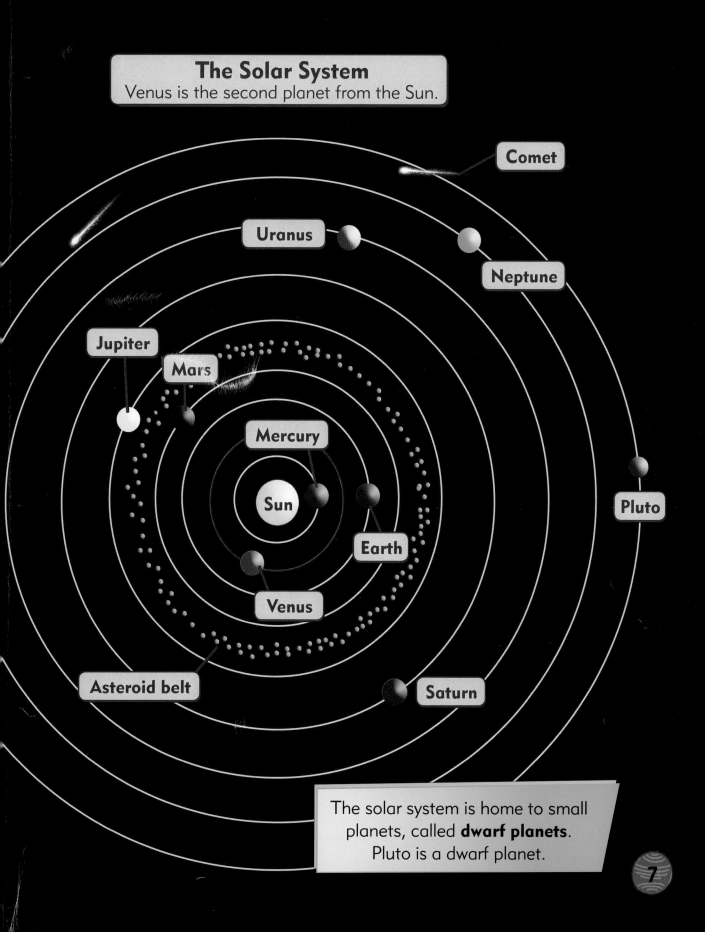

The Solar System

Venus is the second planet from the Sun.

Comet

Uranus

Neptune

Jupiter

Mars

Mercury

Sun

Earth

Venus

Pluto

Asteroid belt

Saturn

The solar system is home to small planets, called **dwarf planets**. Pluto is a dwarf planet.

Venus's Amazing Journey

The time it takes a planet to **orbit**, or circle, the Sun once is called its year.

Earth takes just over 365 days to orbit the Sun, so a year on Earth lasts 365 days.

Venus is closer to the Sun than Earth, so it makes a shorter journey.

It takes Venus about 225 Earth days to orbit the Sun.

This means that a seven-year-old on Earth would be 11 in Venus years!

As a planet orbits the Sun, it also spins, or **rotates**, like a top. Earth takes 24 hours to rotate once. Venus spins very slowly and takes 243 Earth days to rotate once.

Venus

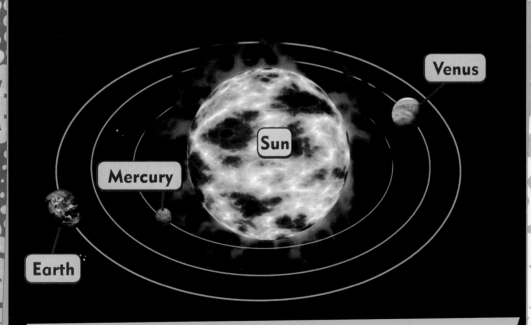

If you could look at Venus from above the planet, you would see that it rotates in a clockwise direction. Most planets rotate in a counterclockwise direction.

To orbit the Sun once, Earth makes a journey of about 584 million miles (940 million km). Venus makes a journey of about 422 million miles (680 million km).

A Closer Look at Venus

Venus is the closest planet to Earth.

You don't need a telescope to see Venus—you can see it just with your eyes!

From Earth, Venus is the brightest planet in the solar system.

It looks so bright because of its covering of thick, yellowish-white clouds.

The Sun's light reflects, or bounces, off the clouds, making the planet shine.

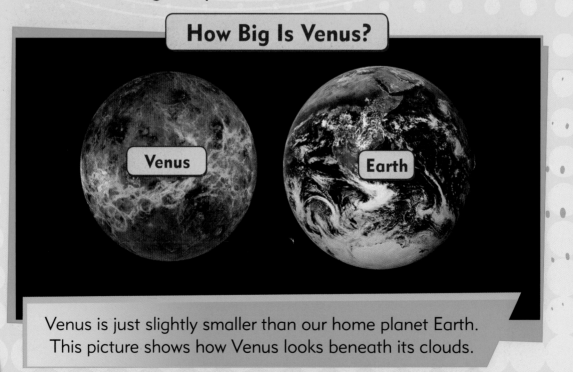

How Big Is Venus?

Venus

Earth

Venus is just slightly smaller than our home planet Earth. This picture shows how Venus looks beneath its clouds.

The Moon

Venus

This photo of Venus was taken from Earth. Venus can often be seen shining in the sky just before sunrise or just after sunset.

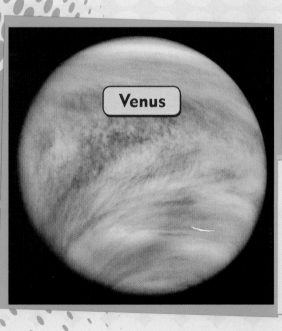

Venus

This photo of Venus's thick clouds was taken by a spacecraft. The top layer of clouds is blown around the planet by winds that are as powerful as a hurricane!

Deadly Venus

Our home planet, Earth, is covered with a thick layer of gases called an **atmosphere**.

These gases include **oxygen**, which is the gas that humans and other animals need to breathe.

Like Earth, Venus also has a thick atmosphere.

You couldn't breathe on Venus, though, because the planet's atmosphere is toxic.

Venus's atmosphere is deadly in another way, too.

It's so heavy, it would crush you in less than a second!

Venus is the hottest planet in the solar system. Day and night it is so hot, that some metals would melt on the planet's surface!

Once heat from the Sun reaches the surface of Venus, it stays there! That's because the thick atmosphere keeps it trapped on the planet.

The Sun

Clouds

Atmosphere

Venus

What's Beneath ☆☆ the Clouds?

It's not possible to see through Venus's thick clouds and atmosphere using a telescope.

So scientists use **radar equipment** that sends **radio waves** to the planet.

The radio waves bounce off the planet's surface and carry information back to computers on Earth.

Using radar, scientists found out that Venus has a mountain that is 7 miles (11 km) high.

That's taller than Mount Everest, the tallest mountain on Earth!

The mountain is named Maxwell Montes (MAX-well MON-tez).

Scientists used information collected by radar to create these pictures of Venus's surface.

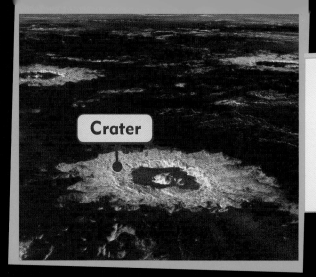

Crater

This picture shows a **crater** on Venus. Large space objects, such as asteroids, hit Venus's surface and make craters that are many miles wide.

Maat Mons

This picture shows Venus's tallest volcano. It is 5 miles (8 km) high. The volcano is called Maat Mons (MAHT MONZ).

Missions to Venus

In 1962, a spacecraft called *Mariner 2* flew past Venus and beamed information back to Earth.

It was the first spacecraft to ever travel to another planet!

Since then, more than 20 spacecraft have flown to Venus to study the planet.

Some of them actually landed on the planet's surface.

The spacecraft were soon destroyed by the heat, though, or crushed by the weight of Venus's atmosphere!

This is a *Venera* spacecraft. Several *Venera* spacecraft landed on Venus. One survived on the planet's surface for 110 minutes. Then it was melted and crushed!

Mariner 2

This is *Mariner 2*. It discovered that Venus rotates in the opposite direction than Earth and most other planets.

Exploring Venus

In May 1989, a spacecraft named *Magellan* was carried into space aboard the space shuttle *Atlantis*.

Once *Magellan* was in space, it separated from *Atlantis* and flew to Venus.

Magellan orbited Venus and studied the planet for four years.

The final part of its mission was to fly into the planet's atmosphere.

Magellan sent information about Venus's atmosphere back to Earth until it burned up!

Magellan

Scientist

This photo shows scientists working on *Magellan*.

Blue areas are low ground.

Green areas are medium-height places.

Pinkish-brown areas are high places, such as mountains.

This picture of Venus was created by *Magellan* using radar. The colors have been added on a computer to show the different heights of the land.

This is *Venus Express*, which went into orbit around Venus in 2006. It has discovered that volcanoes on Venus may be erupting today.

19

Venus Fact File

Here are some key facts about Venus, the second planet from the Sun.

Discovery of Venus

Venus can be seen in the sky without a telescope. People have known it was there since ancient times.

How Venus got its name

The planet is named after the Roman goddess of love and beauty.

Planet sizes

This picture shows the sizes of the solar system's planets compared to each other.

Sun · Mercury · Earth · Venus · Mars · Jupiter · Saturn · Uranus · Neptune

Venus's size

7,521 miles (12,104 km) across

How long it takes for Venus to rotate once

243 Earth days

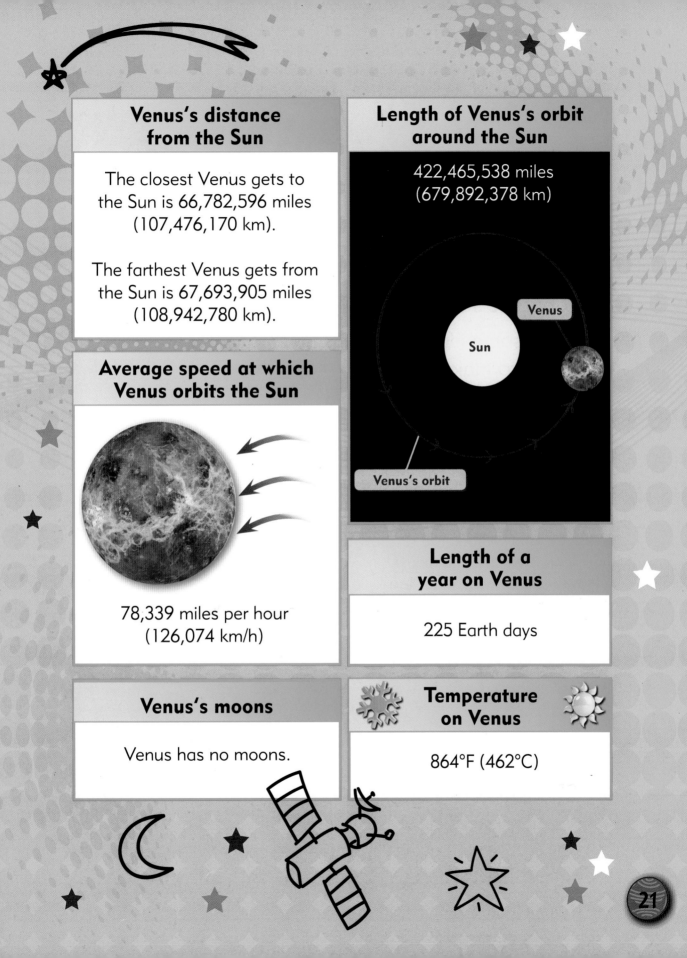

Venus's distance from the Sun

The closest Venus gets to the Sun is **66,782,596** miles (107,476,170 km).

The farthest Venus gets from the Sun is **67,693,905** miles (108,942,780 km).

Length of Venus's orbit around the Sun

422,465,538 miles (679,892,378 km)

Venus

Sun

Venus's orbit

Average speed at which Venus orbits the Sun

78,339 miles per hour (126,074 km/h)

Length of a year on Venus

225 Earth days

Venus's moons

Venus has no moons.

Temperature on Venus

864°F (462°C)

Get Crafty
Make a Hot and Toxic Collage

Create a collage picture that shows how Venus's atmosphere and clouds block out the Sun.

Here are some ideas for things you could use to make a collage:

- Scraps of colored paper or cardboard
- Tissue paper or giftwrap paper

Here's one example of a Venus collage, but you can create your own hot and toxic world! Think about:

- What colors will you use to show the poisonous gas around Venus?
- How will you make Venus look scorching hot?

Here are some items you might need when making your collage:

- A large sheet of thin cardboard or construction paper for the background
- Scissors
- White glue
- A paintbrush for spreading glue
- An adult to help with cutting

Glossary

asteroid (AS-teh-royd) A large rock that is orbiting the Sun. An asteroid can be as small as a car or bigger than a mountain.

atmosphere (AT-muh-sfeer) A layer of gases around a planet, moon, or star.

comet (KAH-mit) A space object made of ice, rock, and dust that is orbiting the Sun.

crater (KRAY-tur) A bowl-shaped hole in the ground. Craters are often caused by asteroids and other large, rocky objects hitting the surface of a planet or moon.

dwarf planet (DWARF PLAN-et) A round object in space that is orbiting the Sun. Dwarf planets are much smaller than the eight main planets.

gas (GASS) A substance, such as oxygen or helium, that does not have a definite shape or size.

orbit (OR-bit) To circle, or move around, another object.

oxygen (OX-ih-jin) An invisible gas in the air that you and other living things need to breathe.

planet (PLAN-et) A large object in space that is orbiting the Sun. Some planets, such as Venus, are made of rock. Others, such as Jupiter, are made of gases and liquids.

radar equipment (RAY-dahr ee-KWIP-munt) Machines that produce radio waves. When radio waves bounce off an object, they can be used to figure out information such as the size and shape of that object.

radio wave (RAY-dee-oh WAVE) An invisible wave that travels through the air and can carry out different tasks. For example, your TV remote control sends radio waves to the TV to change the channel.

rotate (ROH-tate) To spin around.

solar system (SOH-ler SIS-tem) The Sun and all the objects that orbit it, such as planets, their moons, asteroids, and comets.

toxic (TOX-ik) Poisonous.

volcano (vol-KAY-noh) A mountain or hill that has an opening on it from which hot, liquid rock can erupt onto the surface of a planet or another body in space.

Index

Read More

Howard, Fran. *Venus (Planets)*. Edina, MN: ABDO Publishing (2008).

Hughes, Catherine D. *First Big Book of Space (National Geographic Little Kids)*. Washington, D.C.: The National Geographic Society (2012).

Learn More Online

To learn more about Venus, go to
www.rubytuesdaybooks.com/venus